SO-AXX-913

ADVENTURE CAT!

And More True Stories of Amazing Cats!

Kathleen Weidner Zoehfeld

NATIONAL
GEOGRAPHIC

WASHINGTON, D.C.

Copyright © 2018 National Geographic Partners, LLC

Published by National Geographic Partners, LLC.
All rights reserved. Reproduction of the whole or any
part of the contents without written permission from
the publisher is prohibited.

Since 1888, the National Geographic Society has
funded more than 12,000 research, exploration, and
preservation projects around the world. The Society
receives funds from National Geographic Partners,
LLC, funded in part by your purchase. A portion of
the proceeds from this book supports this vital work.
To learn more, visit natgeo.com/info.

NATIONAL GEOGRAPHIC and Yellow Border
Design are trademarks of the National Geographic
Society, used under license.

For more information, visit nationalgeographic.com,
call 1-800-647-5463, or write to the following address:

National Geographic Partners
1145 17th Street N.W.
Washington, D.C. 20036-4688 U.S.A.

Visit us online at nationalgeographic.com/books

For librarians and teachers: ngchildrensbooks.org

More for kids from National Geographic:
kids.nationalgeographic.com

For information about special discounts for bulk
purchases, please contact National Geographic Books
Special Sales: specialsales@natgeo.com

For rights or permissions inquiries, please contact
National Geographic Books Subsidiary Rights:
bookrights@natgeo.com

Designed by Ruth Ann Thompson

National Geographic supports K–12
educators with ELA Common Core
Resources. Visit natgeoed.org/
commoncore for more information.

Trade paperback ISBN: 978-1-4263-3052-0
Reinforced library edition ISBN: 978-1-4263-3053-7

Printed in China
17/RRDS/1

Table of CONTENTS

SKATTY: A SHIP'S CAT!

Skatty hangs on to Paul Thompson's sailboat with his special paws.

A cat can be "man's best friend," too!

Chapter 1

THE PERFECT KITTEN

Paul Thompson's smartphone beeped. A text message had come in. Even though the phone was right next to him, Paul didn't notice the sound. But his new kitten did. The curious kitten reached out his big white paw and patted the screen. Paul looked up from his work and spotted the new text. He couldn't help but smile. This new kitten was going to be a big help!

When he was very young, Paul got sick with German measles and whooping cough at the same time. After that, he began to lose his hearing. By the time he was six, one ear was completely deaf, and he had only a little hearing in the other. He wore a hearing aid and got good at lip reading. A speech teacher taught him how to speak clearly.

When he was just 11 years old, growing up in East London, South Africa, he met a boy his own age down on the docks in the harbor. The boy had been sailing on a yacht with his family and was just passing through. But he and Paul quickly became friends. They talked about the thrill of sailing across the vast blue ocean. Ever since that day, Paul says, he's dreamed of sailing single-handed around the world.

Today Paul works as a computer programmer. Besides working hard at his job, Paul has another goal—to get as much sailing experience as he can. In 1994, he became the first deaf person to sail across the southern Atlantic Ocean by himself. "Deaf people," he said, "can do everything except hear. We prove that every day." But it doesn't hurt to have a little help from a kitty cat! When he sailed the Atlantic, he had a ship's cat—a gray tabby named Tommy. Tommy lived to be 20 years old. Paul missed Tommy very much.

He wanted a new cat who would be a good companion on his long journey around the world.

Today, Paul lives in Auckland, New Zealand. As a sailor, Paul had always admired Maine coon cats. In general, cats don't like water. If you've ever tried to give your cat a bath, you probably discovered how much they hate it! But Maine coons are actually known to like water! He looked at all the rescue centers nearby, hoping to find one who needed a new home. There were none to be found. So, he decided to contact a special Maine coon cat breeder. In the world of pet cats,

Did You Know?

Maine coon cats are the largest of all house cat breeds. The biggest males can weigh up to 33 pounds (15 kg). The largest females reach up to 22 pounds (10 kg).

a breeder is someone who chooses the mother and father cats, based on their special traits. Those traits are passed down to their kittens.

The name of one local breeder's business caught his attention: It was RebelPawz. Why "RebelPawz"? This breeder had a special interest in polydactyl (sounds like PAH-lee-dack-tuhl) cats. "Poly" means "many." And "dactyl" refers to fingers or toes. Polydactyl kitties have extra toes on each paw. Every year, a few of RebelPawz's kittens are born with this trait. For the owners of most purebred Maine coon cats, having extra toes isn't desired. But for some, it's welcome!

Cat Super Senses #1
Super Hearing

Compared to humans, cats have super hearing. Their ears are tuned in to sounds that no human ears can hear, such as the high-pitched squeaks of mice. Even if a mouse doesn't squeak, a cat can hear it rustling through grass or leaves. Not only that, but they can tell different types of rodents (such as mice, voles, moles, or rats) apart by the squeaks and other sounds they make.

And those upright, pointy ears are not just cute! Cats can swivel their ears—each one in a different direction if necessary—to pinpoint the exact location of a mouse or other prey.

These cats were a favorite on ships. "Old-time sailors believed that the big paws gave them a better grip on the deck," said Paul. "And they say it also made them better mousers." So, for a ship's cat, being polydactyl is a helpful trait.

Paul went to visit the breeder. Her name was Marie. Marie told him that both of her mother cats were due to have kittens in nine weeks. It felt like a long wait. But at last the day came when Paul could go and visit the new kittens. There were 10 of them! He could hardly believe how lovely and charming they all were. He asked Marie to help him decide which one should be his.

"She knew that I'd be taking my kitten sailing and that we'd have many interesting

adventures together," said Paul. Marie didn't hesitate. She knew her kittens well. She pointed out the red tabby with the big white paws.

The kitten's father was born in Vienna, Austria. So, Marie had named him Strauss (sounds like STROWSS), after Johann (sounds like YO-hahn) Strauss, the famous music composer from Vienna. The name warmed Paul's heart. When he was growing up, one of his favorite songs was Strauss's waltz "The Blue Danube." Today Paul's hearing is gone completely. "The worst thing about my ears now," he said, "is—no more music. Everything else is not

a problem. But that's the part that hurts."
He wishes he could remember more music,
but he still hears that beautiful Strauss
melody in his head.

Paul counted the little red kitten's toes.
Seven on each front paw, and five on each
hind paw. A true polydactyl! Strauss was
perfect. Some people say that in picking a
cat, there's just a little bit of fate involved.
To Paul, it certainly seemed as if this match
was meant to be.

Paul added "von Skattebol" to his new
kitten's name. *Skattebol* means "my
darling" or "my treasure" in Afrikaans,
Paul's second language.
A kitten from a breeder
has what's called a
pedigree. That means the

Did You Know?

Non-polydactyl cats
have five toes on each
front paw and four toes
on each hind paw.

names of his parents and grandparents and great-grandparents are carefully recorded. A pedigreed cat's name must include its breeder's name. At first, "Strauss von Skattebol of RebelPawz" seemed like a comically long name for such a small bit of fluff. But he knew his kitten would grow into his big name soon enough. Paul nicknamed him "Skatty."

Maine coon cats are known to be calm, intelligent, and caring. Most love cuddling and sticking close by their owners. Some of the most outgoing among them work as comforting therapy cats for people sick in hospitals, or for elderly folks in nursing homes.

"I'm totally deaf, and Skatty is my ears," said Paul. When someone knocks at the door, Skatty tries to get Paul's attention and walks to the door. "Without any training, Skatty caught on that I don't hear. Skatty learned to get my attention by coming and putting his paw on my knee. And I've learned to get up and follow him. Normally that leads to his food bowl (empty!). But often enough, it's something I'm glad to know about!"

Skatty was certainly an adorable and helpful kitten. But would he have the right temperament to be happy and content on a long sail around the world?

Skatty gets used to being on a moving sailboat.

Chapter 2

A PROPER SEA CAT

Many cats get nervous in any kind of moving vehicle. But ever since the day Paul and Skatty first drove home together, Skatty was comfortable riding in the car. "Skatty is the most amazing cat I've ever had in the car," said Paul. "He never gets fussy, no matter what happens." For Paul, this was a reassuring sign that Skatty would like his new home.

"Home" was Paul's beautiful 32-foot (9.8-m)-long sailboat named *La Chica* (sounds like LAH CHEE-kah). Skatty began his sea cat training that first day, by simply spending time on *La Chica* with his new "cat dad." They stayed in dock. Paul didn't try to start the engine or hoist the sails. He wanted Skatty to get used to the boat first. The kitten was curious and wanted to explore everything!

During the winter months, Paul divides his time between *La Chica* and his Auckland apartment. Even in the apartment, Skatty soon demonstrated the Maine coon's love of water. "He always wants to play in the sink," said Paul. "If he's bored I'll turn on the tap for him, and he'll play at catching the water with his paws. As the sink fills up, he's perfectly happy to sit there in the water while he plays."

On the sailboat, though, that curiosity about water could get him in big trouble. Paul was worried that Skatty might fall overboard. He had to keep an eye on the little kitty all the time. And it's a good thing he did! One day, Skatty seemed more determined than ever to get a better view of the water. "He climbed out on the bumpkin," said Paul. "That's the metal frame at the back of the boat that holds the steering gear. It juts out over the water. And it's made of stainless steel pipe, so it's very slippery." Skatty's special paws may give him a good grip on deck, but no paws are wide enough to hold a cat on a slippery bumpkin! Splash! Down he went.

"I was expecting it," said Paul, "so I was on hand and ready to rescue him. It must have been quite a shock when he hit the water. But he kept his wits about him and didn't panic. He swam to the rudder. And he hauled himself up on a flat part of it, which was just a few inches under the water. There he calmly waited for me to rescue him."

The boat's dinghy (sounds like DING-ee), or smaller rowboat, was in the water behind them, attached by a long rope. Paul quickly pulled the dinghy up beside the rudder, and Skatty climbed in. He pulled the dinghy up close to the sailboat, and Skatty jumped back on board.

A Long Tradition of Cats at Sea

No one knows exactly when humans first began keeping cats as pets. But Egyptian murals from more than 3,000 years ago show cats helping people hunt birds from their Nile River boats. And there's evidence that cats may have sailed on Viking ships more than 1,000 years ago.

The first cats to sail long distances were probably on board to provide an important service: pest control! Mice and rats can chew right through ships' ropes and get into the food supply. A ship's cat helped solve the pest problem, while providing fun and a friend for the crew.

"He'd only been in the water for about two minutes, but it was cold!" said Paul. He dried Skatty off and wrapped him in a towel. The two of them sat by the heater together for a couple of hours. Paul was very proud of how brave his kitten had been after the fall. And the kitten behaved perfectly for the rest of the day!

After about two months, Skatty seemed to be feeling completely at home on the boat. Paul decided it was time to give Skatty his first taste of sailing. They spent a week sailing around the Hauraki (sounds like how-RAH-kee) Gulf, close to home.

For safety while they were underway, Skatty wore a harness and leash.

Although Skatty quickly adjusted to living on the boat while in dock, it took a while for him to get used to sailing. At first, the roar of the engine startled him—a boat's engine is a lot noisier than a car's! On the first day out, the rocking of the boat made him seasick. Poor Skatty! Cats can get seasick and throw up just like people can.

Paul prefers Skatty to ride safely in his lap or by his side when they are sailing. "That will change later," he said, remembering his hardened sea cat, Tommy, who was allowed to use his own judgment, when walking on deck. "But for now, I have to protect Skatty from his own impulsive self." Once he's totally comfortable with sailing, the harness will be set aside. In the meantime, Skatty looks quite handsome wearing it!

As to whether Skatty is a good mouser, that has yet to be tested. But on sunny days, he loves to sit on deck and watch everything that's going on. He seems to have his heart set on catching a pesky seagull. But so far, he's had no luck with that!

When it's time to rest, he especially likes sitting on the solar panels. "They keep his bottom warm," said Paul, but it's hard for solar panels to generate electricity if they are blocked by a cat. In rough weather, Skatty usually sleeps "down below" in the cabin, under the table.

Paul built his boat himself. He chose a classic sailboat design created in 1932 by the American boat designer John Hanna, who, like Paul, was deaf.

For Skatty, that's the most comfortable spot on the boat. At night, however, Skatty likes to sleep next to Paul in his bunk, curled up in the crook of his knee.

During the day when they're docked, Paul sets up his computer on the table and gets some work done. "When people come alongside, or other boats go past, Skatty is alert, and he starts looking around," said Paul. "If he knows the boat, he'll get my attention and go outside—which for me is wonderful, because when I sit down below, I have no idea what's happening on deck. Skatty's a big help! For the first time, when people come visit me, I can actually come out and be sociable."

Skatty keeps watch as he and Paul get ready to set sail.

Chapter 3

PLANNING FOR THE BIG JOURNEY

As they get ready for the big trip, Paul and Skatty have a lot to do. An around-the-world sail takes a lot of planning! "First," said Paul, "I did a few things to make *La Chica* safer for Skatty." He started by putting some netting under that bumpkin!

In case Skatty does fall in again, Paul trails a thick rope behind the boat for him to climb up.

Among the list of other things that Skatty will need: plenty of good food, of course. When they're out sailing for a few days in a row, Paul stocks up on the type of wet cat food that comes in pouches.

Then there's the big bag of pine pellets for his litterbox. Like any good ship's cat, Skatty's litter box is in the "head." That's what sailors call the bathroom.

Although a cat will sleep just about anywhere he chooses, it's important to have a special, soft and cozy cat bed for catnaps. Also, he'll want plenty of toys to play with and a bit of cat grass to chew on when his tummy's not feeling quite right.

Every cat needs a scratching post as well, and ships' ropes make some of the

finest scratching
post material.
Paul wrapped
and glued rope to
the base of one mast.
That turned out to be
the perfect scratching post.
Ship's cat–approved!

Paul built a special cat flap in the main door to the cabin, too. That way, when they're docked, Skatty can go up on deck or down below whenever he pleases. The "door" has a special part that seals it against big waves during stormy weather. As they cross the globe, Paul and Skatty are sure to run into a lot of that!

Skatty has his own life vest for when the seas get rough, too. Paul had to make the vest himself, though. You can buy life vests for small dogs, but none of them work very well for cats.

Once all the supplies and safety features were in place, Paul decided it was time for their first long trip. After six weeks of sailing, stopping in many different ports around New Zealand, Skatty had gotten his sea legs. He grew from a curious, accident-prone kitten into a true sea cat!

If they could, Paul and Skatty would love to spend all their time on *La Chica*. But, of course, that's not possible. When they're not on board, Paul takes Skatty with him almost everywhere. Skatty was so quick to understand Paul's hearing loss that Paul wondered if Skatty would be a good therapy cat. Would he have the calm and outgoing personality needed to cheer up folks in hospitals or nursing homes? No cat can be registered as a therapy cat until it is at least one year old. If Skatty were ever going to be a therapy cat, Paul knew it was important to expose him to new experiences gradually as he grew up.

A good therapy cat should be intelligent and easy to train. He should be calm in unfamiliar situations and friendly with strangers. Even as young as five and a half months, Skatty showed signs of growing up to be a successful therapy cat.

Did You Know?

Maine coons, Birmans, sphynx, Scottish folds, and Ragdolls are some of the cat breeds most often chosen as therapy cats. But an ordinary house cat can have all the right qualities, too!

Coon Cat Primer

The Maine coon cat is the first breed to be developed in North America, and it is the official cat of the U.S. state of Maine. No one knows exactly how the breed started. But most breeders think it began in New England in the early 1800s, after long-haired European cats left their ships while at anchor. The long-haired cats probably mated with the local short-haired cats, and their kittens became the basis for the coon cat breed.

One thing's for sure—coon cats are not related to raccoons! They do *look* something like raccoons, however, and that is how they got their name.

"The first time we went to a restaurant together for lunch, it was quite noisy with lots of people coming and going," said Paul. "After about half an hour of reacting to everything, he settled down and spent the next two hours calmly on my lap."

Later, they visited a big shopping center in Auckland. "It's a place where a kitty on a leash would be spoken to and sometimes petted by strangers and small children," said Paul. Skatty was a little nervous at first, but he did very well—for a five-and-a-half-month-old kitten at least! He got a bit nervous at the café while Paul waited for his coffee to arrive. So, Paul took him to the nearby library. "I thought that would be a quiet place where he could recover his composure," said Paul. But at the library, they ran into a ladies' knitting group. "They all made a big fuss over him. Which he *mostly* enjoyed!"

A trip to any busy location can be stressful for an inexperienced kitten, but "Skatty coped like the champ he is," said Paul. After all the excitement, Paul took him for a quiet stroll among the stacks in the library, where he finally had a chance to unwind. "All pointers say he is going to be a great therapy cat, among all the other things that he is achieving and doing. Skattebol, my little treasure, is shaping up well."

On their trip around the world, Paul and Skatty will stop in busy ports along the way to visit friends. But there will be long stretches of open sea where man and cat will be alone together. Whether Skatty ends up being a therapy cat or not, having a cat on board, Paul believes, is good therapy for sailors. "It forces you to slow down and take life at your cat's pace. That is a good thing, as we are all far too busy rushing around. Skatty wants to know about everything. As he satisfies his curiosity, I learn to see things in a new light."

Paul is learning to see the world through Skatty's eyes, and Skatty is learning to hear the world for Paul. Together they have developed a very special bond. "Skatty's love is a precious thing to me," says Paul. "Once you earn a cat's love, it is forever. But with a cat, you do have to earn it!"

DUSTY: THE CAT BURGLAR!

When Jean Chu got Dusty, she had no idea he would turn out to be a cat burglar.

Dusty the cat takes a stroll and discovers an interesting object.

Chapter 1

THE MYSTERY OF THE GLOVE ON THE BED

Jean Chu was getting ready for work one morning when she noticed an old glove on the bed. Her husband, Jim, often wore gloves like that when he worked in his workshop. "Jim, don't you think it's time you cleaned up your workshop?" she scolded. She picked up the dirty glove. "And don't bring this grimy stuff upstairs!" She tossed it in the trash.

"It's not *my* glove," Jim replied. "I've never seen it before!"

"Then how did it get on the bed?" Jean wondered. It was a puzzle. Jim told Jean he'd been finding gloves, rags, towels, and other weird things on their front doorstep and in their backyard. "It's been going on for a few weeks," he said. "I've just been picking them up and throwing them away."

Jim suspected their cat, Dusty, was bringing these things home. But it was hard to know for sure. Cats were supposed to bring mice to the doorstep, not gloves!

It all started around the time their next-door neighbors began remodeling their deck. The workers left a few rags and other worn-out or dirty items outside each day.

Had Dusty gotten interested in their trash? And if so, how on earth did he get these things into the backyard? Jim and Jean had fenced in their backyard so their dog would not get out. How could Dusty have possibly gotten over the six-foot (1.8-m)-high fence with a glove in his teeth?

Eventually, Jean found a glove under a bush in the front yard, where she knew Dusty liked to sleep. So, it had to be him!

Every morning, Jim picked up the stuff Dusty had collected during the night and tossed it in the trash. "Maybe we'd better start saving the things he brings home," said Jean. "Maybe he feels he needs to replenish everything."

Jim stopped throwing the things out. But Dusty kept on bringing more things home!

They thought maybe Dusty would stop when the neighbors finished their deck. But after the deck was done, even stranger things began showing up: children's shoes, stuffed animals, bathing suits, socks, and even underwear!

Then one day, a neighbor saw something he could hardly believe. Early one morning he spotted Dusty dragging a towel up the street. "He actually had to drag it walking backward because it was so big," the neighbor told Jean.

It was a long time before Dusty's family caught him in the act. On warm evenings, Jean would sit on the front porch and watch. Finally, one night—there he was—dragging a towel home. There was no getting around it—Dusty was a cat burglar!

He'd been with the family since he was a kitten. When he was growing up, he'd shown no signs of this life of crime that was to come. What had gotten into him? Why was he doing this? Jean and Jim could not figure it out.

The story of how they adopted Dusty is pretty much like anyone's joyful pet adoption story. Jean says that shortly before they got Dusty, Jim surprised their daughters, Kayla and Vanessa, by bringing home a puppy. They named her Daisy, and everyone loved the new puppy. But Jean wanted a new kitten, too. They decided it would be best to get the kitten while Daisy was still a puppy. That way the two could grow up together and learn to be friends.

They went to the Peninsula Humane Society, an animal shelter near their home in San Mateo, California, U.S.A. Jean stayed in the car with Daisy. She told her daughters that she'd love a Siamese (sounds like sigh-ah-MEEZ) kitten, if the shelter had one. After a few minutes, Kayla came out to the car and asked her mom to come in and see the two kittens she liked best.

"The first one was sleeping in the back of its cage," said Jean. "Then Kayla brought me to the other cage, where there were two Siamese kittens who were brothers. She said that every time she went over to their cage, one of them would come over to play with her finger. That one was her other favorite."

Snowshoe Cats

Dusty looks a lot like a Siamese cat—but he has four white paws. That's a rare trait in Siamese, and white boots disqualify a Siamese from official cat shows. Back in the 1960s, one cat breeder decided to try crossing her rare white-booted Siamese cats with two-colored American shorthair cats. Soon, the snowshoe breed was born!

Judging by his white paws, Dusty is probably a snowshoe. All snowshoes have blue eyes and a white V on their muzzles. The V can be big and wide, or as narrow as a simple white streak. As kittens, the fur on their "points"—their ears, face, legs, and tail—is dark, while their bodies are a light creamy color.

Jean thought the playful kitten was adorable. The shelter had a meet-and-greet room where they could get to know the kitten better and introduce him to Daisy. "They didn't play together right away," said Jean, "but Daisy didn't attack the kitten, and the kitten didn't seem to be afraid of the puppy."

As soon as he was out of his cage, the energetic little kitten wandered into every corner and explored under all the chairs. He collected so much dust on his paws and fur, they decided his name should be Dusty.

Dusty was a strong but cuddly kitten who knew how to hold his own with Daisy. From the start, Jean had planned that Dusty would be an indoor cat. But one day, not long after they brought him home, Dusty went missing. "We looked in all his favorite spots," said Jean, "but we couldn't find him anywhere. Out in the backyard, we heard some meowing. We followed the sound and found that he'd gotten locked in Jim's workshop. He must have slipped out through Daisy's doggie door and found his way there."

Dusty's shelter paperwork said he had been an indoor/outdoor kitten, so perhaps he just longed to taste the outdoors again. It was clear to Jean that Dusty was an explorer with a mind of his own. From that time on, she let him come and go as he pleased. His life outdoors was a bit of a mystery, but as far as his family knew, he was just like any ordinary cat, wandering here and there and keeping an eye on the neighborhood.

Dusty sits in a pile of his stolen treasures.

Chapter 2

BURGLAR KITTY EXPOSED!

Looking back, Dusty's skill at fetch might have been a sign to Jim and Jean that their kitten was going to grow up to be a special cat. Jim was the first to discover Dusty's passion. He would shoot a rubber band across the room, and the kitten would chase it down and bring it back to him. "Dusty was better at fetch than Daisy," said Jean. Dusty had incredible focus and speed.

With Daisy, any time they played fetch, Jim would have to wrestle the dog toy from her mouth. But Dusty would just drop his rubber band at Jim's feet and wait for the next launch. Dusty never seemed to tire of playing fetch—that is, until Daisy wanted to play, too! Then Dusty would hop up on a counter. He'd watch scornfully as the goofy puppy ruined the party.

No one knows why Dusty became a cat burglar, but Jean and Jim believe his nightly raids didn't begin until just a few months before he turned two years old. Shortly after Jean caught him dragging the towel home, she began keeping

Did You Know?

The actual term "cat burglar" is used to describe a thief who is as quiet and sneaky as a cat.

a daily journal. She carefully recorded every item Dusty brought home.

"Dusty would leave things all over," said Jean. "He mostly left them by the front steps or in the driveway. Or, he'd leave them in the backyard, even though he had to jump over the fence to do it! But he brought things into the house sometimes, too. He'd line items up on the floor in the dining room or kitchen. He'd bring little toys into our daughters' room."

"Once, one of our daughters had a sleepover. Everyone slept in the living room. In the morning, there were four or five things lined up, almost as if he was bringing a present for each of the girls," laughed Jean.

Cat Super Senses #2
Super Vision and Whisker Touch

During the day, cats don't see as well as humans do. But at night, they have super vision! Whether you're a cat or a human, light gets into your eyes through your pupils. Those are the dark areas at the center of each eye. Pupils open wide in dim light, and they shrink in bright light. Cats' pupils are long and slit-like, and they can open more than three times as wide as a human's! Even if there is only a tiny bit of light, a cat's pupils can take it in.

Cats have good distance vision, but they have a harder time focusing on things that are right up close. That's where whiskers come in handy. Cats can swing their whiskers forward to get a clear "touch picture" of objects in front of their noses.

As Jean kept her journal, the list of things Dusty stole grew longer and more hilarious. Jean says that one of the funniest things was a child's umbrella. The scariest thing was probably a small striped snake. At first she thought it was a girl's headband and nearly picked it up! One morning Jim found a bikini top on the doorstep. The next morning, he found the bottom. One night, Dusty dragged home four towels, four socks, a small mesh bag, a potholder, and a yellow glove. That was a record! Jean's list just kept growing: balloons, sponges, car-washing mitts, soccer shoes, a pair of flippers for scuba diving, various pool toys, and a birthday party goodie bag. You name it, Dusty would take it!

When a neighbor decided to remodel his home, it was a bonanza for Dusty. One night, he dragged home two bags of bolts. Each bag weighed almost a pound (0.5 kg)! Jean returned the bolts to the builders. "One of them said he'd spent thirty minutes looking for them," said Jean. "After I left, you could hear them laughing from all the way down the street."

Jean is a dentist, and Dusty soon became a big topic of conversation at her office. She began bringing Dusty's treasures in to show her staff. "My patients loved seeing what he'd taken, too," said Jean. "It was always: 'What did he get this time?' At the end of each day, I'd just toss it all into a pile in the corner of my office."

As the pile
of loot grew,
Jean spotted an
interesting article in a
magazine. It was about
a cat in England that began
bringing stuffed animals home
after her owners had a new baby.
"Hey," she thought, "Dusty brings home
WAY more stuff than that." She contacted
the magazine.

Dusty didn't get into the magazine, but
he did get a short article on the magazine's
pet website. Then, a few months later,
Jean got a call from the television channel
Animal Planet. They were making a new
show called *Must Love Cats*. They'd read
the online article about Dusty and wanted

to know if Jean would like him to be on their show.

By that time, Dusty had stolen more than 600 different items. But apart from a couple of brief sightings, no one *really* knew how he did it. John, the show's host, suggested they set up a night vision camera near the front door. They'd try and catch Dusty in the act!

For the next two weeks, John's video camera rolled, while Dusty prowled the neighborhood. "Night after night, Dusty slips into the darkness, looking to raid the possessions of his unsuspecting neighbors," the show began. What the camera revealed amazed Jean and her family.

"I've never seen him like that!" cried Jean as she watched the first clips of

Dusty bringing home a towel, swim goggles, a sponge, and a glove!

"He is a busy kitty," said John.

"This cat is so funny to me," Jean laughed as she watched him trotting along with a stuffed dinosaur in his teeth. "He needs therapy! Or he gets arrested—one or the other!"

The show aired on a Saturday night. The following week, Jean figured her staff and some of her patients would tease her about the show. They'd all have a good laugh, and that would be the end of it. But the video of Dusty's exploits was a huge hit. That Monday, Jean and Jim were invited to be on a local television talk show. Jean and Jim were surprised there would be that much interest in their special cat.

Dusty sizes up an interesting object.

Chapter 3

PAYING FOR HIS CRIMES

The next day, a local television reporter asked if he could do a story on Dusty for the San Francisco evening news. The station's network headquarters in New York decides which news stories to send to their other stations around the country. To Jean and Jim's amazement, nearly all the network's stations across the country were suddenly airing Dusty's story.

Dusty and his whole family were then invited to New York City, to be guests on a popular television talk show. He became the subject of many radio interviews and was featured in newspapers and magazines around the world. He even ended up in the bonus section on the DVD of the movie *Puss in Boots*. Almost overnight, Dusty had become famous.

The fame didn't go to Dusty's head, though. After all, deep down, he is still just a regular cat. What he loves most is having his family around him, a comfy cat bed to sleep in by day, a nice bowl of kibble for supper, and the familiar doggie door to slip out of by night.

Over time, Dusty's neighbors have gotten to know him well. "I've gone to them so many times, asking if any of these items belong to them. When something goes missing from their

Did You Know?

Cats are natural hunters. Cat behavior experts say that, in cities where cats can't find much living prey, at least a few may turn to "hunting" other things!

yards, they know who to call," laughs Jean.

At one point, the pile of stolen goods had gotten so high, Jean decided to hold a "reverse garage sale." She washed and folded the towels and the pieces of clothing that were in good shape. She sorted all the toys and tools and other useful items. Then she invited the neighbors in to have a look and take home what was theirs.

What the neighbors didn't claim, she brought to a big fund-raiser at the adoption center where the family first met and adopted Dusty. "This was Dusty's transitional home," said Jean, "where they gave him lots of love, until he rescued us.

They do such wonderful work, we wanted to help them out."

Jean made a cute black-and-white-striped "jailbird" outfit for Dusty. He seemed to like the costume, and it suited him well! Since Dusty had become a big star, everyone was eager to meet him and get their picture taken with him. Many came to shake his paw, scratch him behind his ears, and leave a donation for the shelter. Donors got to take home one of Dusty's stolen towels. Jean had embroidered Dusty's name and paw print on each one. In this way, Dusty could use his fame to help many animals find loving homes and forever families, just like he did.

Besides taking part in the fund-raiser, Dusty was asked to be the grand marshal of the annual Pet Parade in the nearby city of Burlingame (sounds like BUHR-ling-game). In his workshop, Jim designed and built a "portable prison cell" on wheels for Dusty to ride in. The door to the cell was held shut with a big padlock labeled "Dusty." The famous kitty dressed up in his jailbird suit for the big occasion. He glared proudly at all the curious dogs who came by his cell to sniff him and look him over.

Later, Dusty even made a special visit to some people who were sick in a hospital. A chaplain (sounds like CHAP-lin) from a local hospital had one patient who especially loved Dusty. The chaplain contacted Jean to see if Dusty could come and visit all of her patients. Jean said, "Dusty is such a good cat. He didn't mind being petted and cuddled by everyone." The hospital welcomed the little burglar in. And he behaved like an angel.

Despite all the responsibilities that come with fame, Dusty still finds time to go out searching for treasure at night. The neighbors know his habits. Children no longer leave their shoes and toys laying around outside at night. "Instead of toys, Dusty now picks up the trash—fast food wrappers, grocery bags, things like that," said Jean. "He's doing his part to clean up the neighborhood."

Dusty is a very good cat, indeed!

Adopt a Shelter Kitty

More than three million cats and kittens end up at animal shelters in the United States every year. If you are ready to provide a safe and comfortable environment for a new pet, try going to your local ASPCA (American Society for the Prevention of Cruelty to Animals) or Humane Society first. Many cats are waiting there for their forever homes. The shelter will help you get the vaccinations your cat needs to stay healthy. Spaying or neutering your new kitty is a good idea, too. That will help insure there will be fewer unwanted kittens crowding the shelters in the future!

Vladimir's leash keeps him close to his owners as he takes on the world.

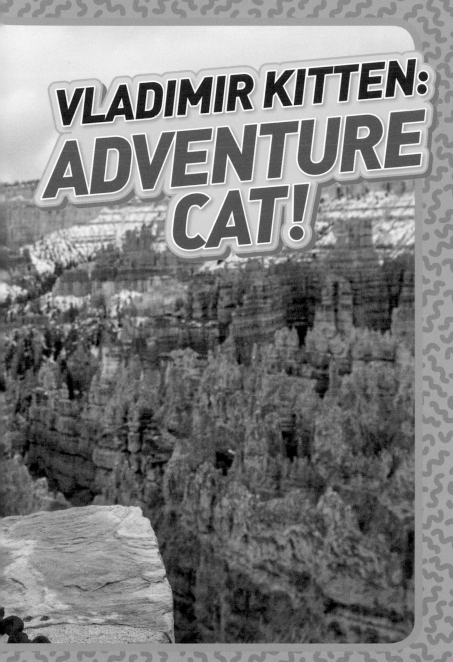

VLADIMIR KITTEN: ADVENTURE CAT!

Vladimir Kitten was born ready for adventure and snow!

Chapter 1

AN ADVENTURE KITTEN IS BORN

One day, in a small town in Utah, U.S.A., a tiny white kitten was born. He had a black tail and a cute little black spot on top of his head. The kitten and his siblings drank their mother's milk and grew. They snuggled up together and slept. At a week old, the kitten's eyes opened, and he took in the world. At three weeks, he began learning to walk on wobbly legs.

When he turned five weeks old, he began trying out his jumping and pouncing skills. He ran and pounced and played. But the kitten didn't have a real home. He and his brothers and sisters lived outside. One day, a nice lady found them. She put an ad online to help them find homes.

Madison Hofman spotted the ad and couldn't believe her luck. Those kittens needed homes, and she desperately wanted a kitten!

Madison and her new husband, Cees (sounds like CASE), had just graduated from college. They both loved hiking, climbing, and exploring. They agreed that before they settled down, they would go on one great big outdoor adventure. They would fix up an old recreational vehicle (or RV) and travel around the country, stopping at every national park. The United States has 59 national parks, so that would mean a lot

Did You Know?

The ASPCA has developed a cat personality test that's worked well for helping to match each unique shelter kitty with exactly the right person.

of traveling! Cees figured it would take them about nine months. They had gotten their RV in good shape, and they were almost ready to begin their trip. But Madison felt one important element was still missing in their lives: a cat!

Cees had never been very fond of cats. And the idea of taking a cat on a long trip made him laugh. Like most people, when he thought of traveling pets, he thought of dogs. Cats hate travel, right?! Still, Madison seemed so confident, and she was so insistent (sounds like in-SIS-tent). He decided to make a deal with her.

"Okay," he told her, "but if we're getting a cat, we'll get the cat *today!*"

"It was already after dark, when we had this conversation," Madison remembers. "So Cees probably thought the chances were pretty slim that we'd actually be able to find a kitty that day. But I had already called the lady with the kittens, and I had gotten her address."

Madison quickly stocked up on kitten food, kitty litter, and all the basics for kitten parenting. "I was so excited," said Madison. "I couldn't believe it was actually happening!"

By the time Madison and Cees arrived at the lady's house, there were three kittens that still needed to be adopted. Madison was shocked at how tiny they were. She reached down and scooped one up in her hands. The little white kitten with the spot on his head gazed at her.

"They're all so cute. Which one should I choose?" she asked the lady's young daughter. Before the little girl could answer, two older girls burst through the door and chose the two remaining kittens, right before their eyes.

"Well, that was weird," said Madison. "I guess they helped me decide!"

"The one with the spot is the one I'd have chosen out of all of them, anyway," replied the little girl.

And so, he was theirs. They placed him in a cat carrier and slid it into the car. Madison could see the kitten was scared. She took him out and held him in her lap. "Mew! Mew! Mew!" the kitten cried all the way home. He missed his brothers and sisters. At home, Madison and Cees gave him milk and fed him bits of soft kitten food. They tucked him in bed and stroked his little head. But he cried and cried all night.

The next day, the kitten calmed down, and they got to know each other better. He seemed to like being fussed over and having his picture taken. Both Madison and Cees speak Russian, and they had both lived in Russia for a while as students. So, they agreed their new kitten should have a good, strong Russian name. From now on he would be Vladimir (sounds like VLAD-uh-meer) Kitten!

It was December when they brought their kitten home, and he looked like a tiny little snowball. He was full of energy, too. "He raced around our apartment and climbed to the top of our Christmas tree," laughed Madison. "We took this as an early sign that he wanted to be a climber kitty!"

"Over the next few weeks, we spent so much time with him, he began lying on top of us whenever he slept. He'd pounce on us like a ferocious baby tiger when he was awake, and he'd follow us around all day the rest of the time," said Madison. "I think he quickly decided that we were his new parents."

Not only that, but Vladimir, or "Vlads" as they called him for short, seemed to have won Cees's heart completely. "Cees is very protective of Vlads, and I would constantly catch them doing stuff together," confessed Madison. "I was a little miffed about it at first, since I've always been more of a cat person than Cees, but I could see our kitty totally loved him more! And—out of all the cats in the world—I think Cees loves at least one!"

As Vladimir bonded with his new family, Cees began to see the possibilities of traveling with a cat. Little did the rambunctious (sounds like ram-BUNK-shuss) new kitten know—he was about to go into training for the adventure of a lifetime!

Getting to Know Your Own Special Cat

Before you take your cat on any trip, get to know and respect his or her personality: Is he the type of cat who can't wait to explore new places, or does he take his time getting used to new situations? Does she love to be around you all the time, or does she prefer to do things alone?

Knowing your cat will help you decide if he'll be happiest on a short walk around the backyard, or if he's up for the big family vacation!

Vladimir's handsome red harness helps keep him safe.

Chapter 2

ADVENTURE KITTEN IN TRAINING

The most important thing for any traveling cat is safety. So, as soon as Vladimir was big enough to fit into the smallest-size cat harness, Cees and Madison bought him one. A cat can slip out of a simple collar too easily, and a leash attached to a collar could be dangerous for a cat's soft throat if he's not trained. A harness is safer with straps around two different parts of the body.

Many older cats have a hard time accepting a harness. They may flop on the floor and try to wriggle out of it. But Vladimir was still a kitten when he first wore his. "We practiced putting the harness on him indoors, while he ate his cat food," said Madison. "He hardly even noticed, he was so busy scarfing it down! The food put him in a good mood— so, right away, he began to associate the harness with good experiences."

Over the course of several days, they let Vladimir walk around the house in his harness. "Once he was comfortable with

how it felt, we
went ahead and
attached the
leash and let him
drag it around,"
said Madison.
"Cats are sensitive to
new smells, noises, and
feelings. So, we were careful to
introduce new things to him slowly, and
only when he was in a good mood."

Once Vladimir had gotten a checkup
and all his shots, Cees and Madison took
him out for a stroll in their backyard.
"Then we progressed to a grassy park
near home," said Madison. "We took
everything slowly, and we picked him
up whenever he got scared."

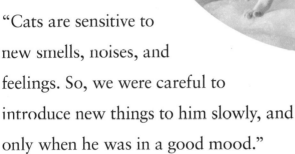

Vladimir quickly learned that the harness and leash meant fun! Not only did he accept the harness, he looked forward to having it on. And Cees and Madison felt good knowing Vladimir could explore, but he'd always be safely within sight.

Before they began their national park journey, they did a lot of research about cat training. When people think about training a new pet to do a few tricks like "sit," "stay," and "come," they almost always think of dogs. Nearly everyone would agree that cats are highly intelligent animals. But most people believe cats are too independent to learn any tricks. Cees and Madison discovered that's not true. It turns out, you can teach a cat to do any tricks a dog can do!

Pets in the Parks

Before you bring your cat to any national or state park, check out its rules regarding pets. You'll find that most of them are written for dogs! But the rules apply to cats as well. They're made to keep your pet safe, as well as to preserve the wild plants and animals of the park. Pets are allowed in certain areas in most parks, but they must be kept on a leash, six feet (2 m) long or less. Or, they can take in the view from the safety of their crate or cat carrier.

"It may sound a little crazy," admitted Madison, "but I couldn't wait to see if Vlads was ready for what I called his 'meowtain cat' training. It was our dream to train him enough to travel everywhere with us, and for him to find the adventure-kitty potential inside himself."

On any outing, even a seasoned adventure cat may accidentally slip out of her harness. Or she may bolt away, because of some frightening sight or sound. So, before starting on any adventure, the first trick a cat must learn is to come when she's called.

A dog will come to you just to make you happy. But a cat is more likely to come if there's food involved! Cees and Madison decided to use a training method many cat behavior experts recommend. Here's how it works:

First, decide on a special sound you want your kitty to respond to. It could be the sound of his or her name. Or you could use a metal clicker. Cees and Madison decided on a whistle. Since they would be in wilderness areas, they needed a loud, clear sound. Vladimir would be able to

Did You Know?

Didga, a rescued shelter kitty from Australia, holds the record for performing the most tricks by a cat in one minute.

hear their whistle, even if he was far away, or if there were other noises in the area.

Then, get your cat used to the sound. If he looks up and moves toward you, even a little, when you make the sound, give him a small tasty treat. Repeat this again and again, each time having him come toward you a little bit longer distance.

The training certainly worked with Vladimir! He soon learned to run to Cees or Madison whenever he heard one of them whistle. "But he doesn't like it much when we forget to have a nice treat ready for him, to tell him what a good kitty he is," laughed Madison. "My advice is to give lots of praise, love, and treats to reinforce good behavior. Vlads knows when we tell him he's a good kitty.

We stroke his back, and he gets all proud and happy!"

Once they were sure Vladimir was ready, they took him on his first short trip. They explored a wild canyon not far from home. "He was still so little," said Madison, "but he hiked and ran along right next to us. He just wanted to be doing whatever we were doing!" They stayed overnight in their cozy RV together, and Vladimir made himself right at home. "Vladimir Kitten," said Madison, "was shaping up to be the cutest, coolest, smartest, best adventure kitty ever!"

Vladimir Kitten poses for a picture on the family RV.

Chapter 3

ON THE ROAD

The new family of three was finally ready to begin a life on the road. Vladimir Kitten was six months old. He loved camping and snuggling up together in the RV. But at first, he didn't like the way it felt when they were moving. "It took him a few days to get used to that," said Madison. "Whenever we were driving, he would come up to the front and sit in one of our laps."

But little Vladimir grew more confident each day. "After a while, he didn't even seem to notice anymore that our house is on wheels!" said Madison.

One thing he seemed to know for sure was that at the end of each drive a big adventure awaited. "Vladimir loves exploring new areas," said Madison. "Every time we open the RV door, he is in an entirely new environment. Some cats might hate the constant change. But Vlads just hops right out, no matter where we are. And he immediately starts exploring."

One of Vladimir's favorite parks was Wrangell-St. Elias (sounds like RANG-ull-saint ee-LIE-us) National Park in Alaska. "Vlads was able to go 'meowtain biking' with us there," said Madison. "He's fascinated by biking and loves to perch on our shoulders when we ride. Cats are such balancing wizards. It's amazing how stable and fearless he is up there!"

Did You Know?

President Theodore Roosevelt, one of the National Park Service's founders, had many pets—among them were two cats: Tom Quartz and Slippers.

He also had the chance to hike up a trail to a glacier (sounds like GLAY-shur) there. And he actually got to walk on it! "When his paws got cold, he rode on our shoulders," said Madison. "The park rangers said he was probably the first cat to ever step foot on Root Glacier. Vlads was pretty proud of that!"

"Parks that have lakes and rivers where you can go kayaking usually allow pets— as long as they stay in the boat with you," said Madison.

Cat Super Senses #3
Super Sniffers

Whenever Vladimir is in a new place, he loves to sniff everything. Vladimir is not alone! Cats are very curious, and they learn a lot about their surroundings through smell. The inside of a cat's nose has more surface area devoted to picking up smells than ours do. It has more than five times as much!

In the wild, cats track their prey by sniffing the scent trails they leave behind. Cats can also tell what other cats have been in the area by detecting the "scent messages" cats leave when they rub their faces on things.

"Vlads has been on kayaking adventures in lots of parks—Yosemite, Mount Rainier, Big Bend, Congaree, and Voyageurs—to name just a few! He's not a big fan of getting wet, so we do everything we can to make sure he doesn't fall in. It has happened a couple of times, though. And he's become a very good swimmer!"

In Acadia National Park in Maine, Vladimir enjoyed the pet-friendly beach. "He especially liked it because the waves weren't too big and scary for him," said Madison. "He dug holes in the sand all day!" In Olympic National Park in Washington, he loved climbing the big rocks on the beach and exploring the piles of driftwood.

And there have been other adventures along the way as well. "The scariest one happened when we were driving from Washington State to Prudhoe Bay in northern Alaska," said Madison. "It took us almost a week to get there. And that was a little too much driving in Vladimir's opinion." The kitten was clearly getting tired of being cooped up for so long. Cees and Madison stopped at Gates of the Arctic National Park for a lunch break. And that's where Vladimir's training paid off for sure!

"We left Vlads asleep on the passenger seat of the RV, and we cracked the window open, just a little bit, since it was a warm day," explained Madison.

"While we were making our sandwiches, he decided to slip out the window and take himself for a walk. We didn't notice he was gone until we'd finished eating. The parking lot was small and surrounded by thick forest. We knew there were all kinds of wild animals out there. We raced through the woods looking for him, whistling and calling his name. After five minutes of sheer panic (which felt more like an hour!), we spotted Vladimir trotting toward us. He was purring and holding his tail straight up the way he does when he's especially happy. He didn't seem concerned at all! We were so relieved to have him back! He got a lot of special treats that day!"

One of Cees and Madison's favorite things about traveling with a cat is the way folks react when they see a cat on a leash.

"Most people are used to seeing dogs out adventuring with their owners," said Madison. "But almost every single person who passes us when we're with Vladimir says: 'Now that's something you don't see every day!' or 'Oh my goodness, a cat on a leash!' Everyone wants their picture taken with Vlads! And he loves posing. He's become a bit of a celebrity, wherever we've gone adventuring.

"As we journeyed around the entire United States, we made sure Vladimir got out to explore in every park. We think he is probably the only cat in the world who has visited so many national parks! In some, he was allowed to hike the trails with us. In all of them, he could at least explore a paved outlook, parking lot, or campground," said Madison. But Vladimir did most of his on-the-ground exploring on pet-friendly trails just outside the national parks. He listened to every rustle, sniffed around every rock and branch, climbed every tree, meandered down every crooked canyon, and stared at every little hidey-hole in the ground.

"Sometimes hikes take twice as long with a kitty companion," said Madison, "but it is fun to slow down, enjoy the moment, and notice more things. When Vlads gets tired, we put him inside one of our backpacks, with his head sticking out, so he can enjoy the view. But it's never long before he meows to let us know he's ready to get down and hike again. It's pretty cute!"

When it comes to exploring, Vladimir is always ready to go! "He still gets a little freaked out when we're in a busy city. There are too many noises and cars. But that's fine with us," declared Madison, "because we aren't really city people anyway." For Cees and Madison, getting to know all our national parks is just the beginning. They plan to keep on traveling in their RV and exploring the great outdoors. And Vladimir won't want to miss a minute of it! Cees and Madison's lonely little rescue kitten has become a brave, world-record-breaking adventure cat. And he is probably very proud of that!

THE END

DON'T MISS!

NATIONAL GEOGRAPHIC KiDS CHAPTERS

TOGETHER FOREVER!

True Stories of Amazing Animal Friendships!

Mary Quattlebaum

Turn the page for a sneak preview . . .

SIRI AND IRIS: BEST MATES!

Cheetah cub Siri plays with her new puppy friend, Iris.

Siri romps through the grass at her new home at the Taronga Western Plains Zoo in Australia.

Chapter 1

Becoming BUDDIES

This was a big day for little Siri. The cheetah cub was about to meet someone special. Her keepers at the Taronga Western Plains Zoo in Australia had planned this moment carefully. Siri's mother had rejected her almost at birth, so the keepers had been caring for the cub at the zoo hospital. But she was all alone. Her keepers knew she needed an animal friend her age to keep her company. They just needed to choose the right buddy.

The new animal trotted over to Siri and sniffed. Wag-wag-wag went her tail. *Let's play!* she seemed to say.

Siri hissed and shrank back. What was this strange black creature? Siri was used to the quiet humans who held her and fed her milk. She didn't know how to deal with a lively puppy. When the pup sniffed again, Siri swatted her. *Stay away!*

Wait a minute! Why put a puppy and a cheetah together? Surely, that friendship was doomed. After all, cheetahs are large members of the cat family. And cats and dogs are enemies, right?

Not always. At other zoos, puppies had been introduced to orphaned cheetah cubs.

Dogs tend to be calm and friendly, and they help calm cheetahs, which can be nervous, timid animals. At the other zoos, the cubs and pups played and slept together, just like siblings. The orphans learned how to behave with other animals, not just with the people who cared for them. The cheetahs wrestled, pounced, and ran with their dog pals. The dogs helped the cubs grow up to be healthy and contented. Then the orphans could get to know the other grown cheetahs at the zoo.

This is important because there are only 10,000 cheetahs left in the world. Through breeding programs at zoos, cheetahs can give birth to cubs and raise them in a safe place. This can help save the species from extinction.

Jen Conaghan, the cheetah supervisor at Taronga Western Plains Zoo, knew about these cub-pup friendships at other zoos. Taronga Western Plains Zoo has a strong breeding program, with nine grown cheetahs. But Jen had never paired a cub with a puppy before. Siri would be the first at the zoo—and in the large country of Australia—to have a puppy pal.

Did You Know?

The cheetah's habitat is shrinking. Today wild cheetahs are found mostly in Africa, but they also used to be found in parts of Asia and the Middle East.

It can take time to make a new friend. Over the next few days, Jen brought the pup for short visits with Siri. The pup was named Iris, which is Siri spelled backward. Maybe that name would bring luck to the friendship.

But Siri continued to hiss and swat. She squealed when Iris came too close. Yet after a time, Jen noticed an important change: Siri began looking for Iris. When the pup came near, she sniffed her. She was becoming less fearful and more curious.

The next step was learning how to play. Because she had no brothers or sisters, Siri had never tussled or tugged. Jen wiggled a soft, blue toy on the floor in front of Siri. Wiggle-wiggle. Siri watched. Like most cats, she naturally wanted to catch a wiggling bit of "prey." She crouched and pounced. She grabbed the toy with her teeth. Jen grabbed the other end . . .

Want to know what happens next? Be sure to check out *Together Forever!* Available wherever books and ebooks are sold.

INDEX

Boldface indicates illustrations.

MORE INFORMATION

To find out more information about the cats featured in this book, ask an adult to check out these Facebook pages, articles, and websites with you:

To follow Skatty and Paul on their adventures, check out their Facebook page: **facebook.com/straussvonskattebol**

To find out what Dusty's been up to lately, check out his Facebook page: **facebook.com/dustythekleptokitty**

To follow Madison and Cees's adventures with Vladimir, read their blog: **ourvie.com**

To learn more about Maine coons and polydactyl cats, visit Rebel-Pawz's website: **rebelpawz.com**

To learn more about the Humane Society: **humanesociety.org**

To learn more about the American Society for the Prevention of Cruelty to Animals (ASPCA): **aspca.org**

For more about our amazing national parks: **nps.gov**

To learn more about cats, read National Geographic "Animals: Domestic Cat": **animals.nationalgeographic.com/animals/mammals/domestic-cat**

For more information about how to have great adventures with your cat: **adventurecats.org**

CREDITS

Cover, Madison Hofman; 4-5, 6, 8, 11, 12, 14, 17, 18, 21, 23, 24, 28, 31, 34, Paul J. Thompson; 38-39, 40, 47, 50, 54, 55, 57, 60, 67, Jean Chu, DDS; 68-69, 70, 75, 79, 80, 82, 83, Madison Hofman; 85, Cees Hofman; 86, Madison Hofman; 89, Cees Hofman; 90, 94, 96, Madison Hofman; 98, Cees Hofman; 102-103, 104, Toby Zerna/Newspix/REX Shutterstock; 111, Jean Chu DDS; 112, Paul J. Thompson

With fond memories of my own feisty little feline, Dusty 2002–2017 —KWZ

ACKNOWLEDGMENTS

Special thanks to: Madison Hofman, Paul Thompson, and Jean Chu for so generously and enthusiastically sharing their amazing kitty cat stories.

And to my wonderful editors, Shelby Alinsky and Souzanne Plasse, photo editor Christina Ascani, and art director Sanjida Rashid—thank you for putting it all together so beautifully!